Encore!
Julian Lloyd Webber

12 Favourites for Cello arranged by
Julian Lloyd Webber and John Lenehan

CHESTER MUSIC
part of The Music Sales Group
14-15 Berners Street, London W1T 3LJ

Cover photograph by Richard Holt

CONTENTS

1.	Jesu, Joy of Man's Desiring	J.S. Bach	2
2.	When I'm Sixty-four	Lennon/McCartney	3
3.	Bess, You is my Woman Now	Gershwin	4
4.	Over the Sea to Skye	Traditional	6
5.	Somewhere (from *West Side Story*)	Bernstein	7
6.	Rondo alla Turca	Mozart	8
7.	Nocturne	Taube	10
8.	Song of the Seashore	Narita	11
9.	Habanera (from *Carmen*)	Bizet	12
10.	Chant Hindu	Rimsky-Korsakov	14
11.	Clair de Lune	Debussy	15
12.	You are my Heart's Delight (from *The Land of Smiles*)	Lehár	18

1. JESU, JOY OF MAN'S DESIRING

J.S. BACH (1685 – 1750)

2. WHEN I'M SIXTY-FOUR

LENNON (1940—1980)
McCARTNEY (b. 1942)

3. BESS, YOU IS MY WOMAN NOW

GERSHWIN (1898 — 1937)

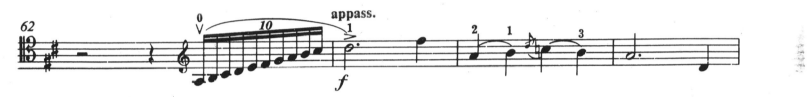

4. OVER THE SEA TO SKYE

TRADITIONAL

5. SOMEWHERE

from *"West Side Story"*

BERNSTEIN (b. 1918)

6. RONDO ALLA TURCA

MOZART (1756–1791)

7. NOCTURNE

EVERT TAUBE (1890—1976)

8. SONG OF THE SEASHORE

NARITA (1893 — 1945)

9. HABANERA

from *"Carmen"*

BIZET (1838 — 1875)

10. CHANT HINDU
(Song of India)

RIMSKY-KORSAKOV (1844 – 1908)

11. CLAIR DE LUNE

DEBUSSY (1862–1918)

morendo jusqu'a la fin

pp

12. YOU ARE MY HEART'S DELIGHT

from *"The Land of Smiles"*

LEHÁR (1870 – 1948)

27

30

mf cresc.

33

pp

36

39 **Tempo primo**

45

49

52

Also available...

Travels with my Cello

A collection of pieces
designed to show off the range and beauty of the cello, arranged for Cello and Piano by

JULIAN LLOYD WEBBER

CONTENTS

1. Golliwog's Cake-Walk — Debussy
2. Adagio — Albinoni/Giazotto
3. Londonderry Air — Traditional
4. Flight of the Bumble Bee — Rimsky-Korsakov
5. Träumerei — Schumann
6. Ave Maria — J.S. Bach/Gounod
7. Puerta de Tierra — Albéniz
8. Andante Affetuoso — W.S. Lloyd Webber
9. The Swan — Saint-Saëns
10. Pizzicato Polka — Strauss
11. Vilja (from *The Merry Widow*) — Lehár
12. Sabre Dance — Khachaturian

The music in this volume is featured on the album
TRAVELS WITH MY CELLO, with Julian Lloyd Webber and the
English Chamber Orchestra conducted by Nicholas Cleobury.

CHESTER MUSIC

Exclusive Distributors:
Music Sales Ltd.
Newmarket Road, Bury St Edmunds, Suffolk IP33 3YB

CD Track Listing and Notes

1. **Jesu, Joy of Man's Desiring**
   The piano plays an eight bar introduction before you come in. Listen out for the crotchet beats in the bass, as this will help you count through the introduction and start in the right place.

2. **When I'm Sixty-Four**
   This piece has a six bar piano introduction.

3. **Bess, You is my Woman Now**
   This piece has a six bar piano introduction.

4. **Over the Sea to Skye**
   This piece has a two bar piano introduction.

5. **Somewhere from *West Side Story***
   This piece starts with four *quaver* clicks before you start- it's slower than you think!

6. **Rondo alla Turca**
   Here, there are three quick *crotchet* clicks and then you are in on the fourth, so watch out!

7. **Nocturne**
   This one has a two bar piano introduction.

8. **Song of the Seashore**
   There are five *quaver* beats here before you start on the sixth, so make sure you are ready!

9. **Habanera from *Carmen***
   This piece has three full bars introduction. You come in on the second beat of the fourth bar.

10. **Chant Hindu**
    Watch out for the piano cue in the first bar, and then count the introduction carefully, before you start in bar 5.

11. **Clair de Lune**
    There are four ***dotted*** crotchet clicks before the piece starts. It begins on a weak beat so count *very* carefully.

12. **You are my Heart's Delight**
    This one has a three bar piano introduction.

Backing tracks programmed by Note-orious Productions Ltd.